COVERT
HYPNOSIS

BY

OLIVER GREGG

COPYRIGHT

© 2014 Oliver Gregg

This book is for information only, its contents are the opinion of the author only.

Use of the information contained within is at the readers discretion.

4

CONTENTS

Introduction.

Congratulations. And thanks for buying this book which has been written to help anyone who wants to improve their relationships in all areas of life.

This book is or anyone you don't have to be a hypnotist or a magician.

You can use it to influence people to make deals go your way, ideal for use in business as well as in your personal life. Start to communicate better and have the upper hand in all conversations.

If you struggle with chatting up members of the opposite sex change that right now. Know how to speak to people in such a way that they will be attracted to you, every time.

The three steps to be used together. Practice using them individually if you need to but to use covert hypnosis effectively you need to use all three together.

About regular hypnosis

The very short version is that hypnosis is a state of mind when, once attained we become more open to suggestion

What covert hypnosis is

Covert hypnosis as the term suggests is the art of creating a hypnotic or suggestible state in another person without them being aware of the fact.

Some rules of the mind.

When you use covert hypnosis or as it is sometimes called conversational hypnosis you will be communicating directly with the subconscious mind.

Your words your posture your actions are all read automatically at a deeper level than most of us realise. Instinctively you might say.

So having an understanding of how this works is fundamental to your success

The subconscious rules

It's not a pleasant thought but even though we think we are in control we are not, we very rarely make conscious decisions based on logic.

The subconscious rules our decisions and it makes decisions based on emotion. Just look at phobias and bad habits for proof of this. A person with a fear of spiders absolutely knows that the tiny creature cannot cause them harm, this is simple logic, but when they see the offending creature they are thrown into panic which is the illogical emotional response.

Same for a smoker, listen to the logical conversation. 'I KNOW I should stop, I KNOW it's harming me, I KNOW it's affecting my kids, I KNOW it's hurting me financially.' All these logical 'I know' yet he or she cannot stop lighting up the next one. Why?

Because the subconscious whirring away in the background out of sight, as the word sub, suggests used emotional reasoning to keep the habit going, it relieves stress and such gobbledygook.

In fact it is so powerful that even when it's completely crazy you cannot stop its power over you.

Just like when a smoker exerts themselves and finds that they are out of breath. 'I can't breathe I need a cigarette!' I have actually heard someone say this.

The subconscious mind does not understand the negative. This means that when you say to someone a statement like "do not think about me" the subconscious actually hears "think about me". Sounds counter intuitive but it's true. For the subconscious to not think about something it has to picture it first.

The classic example is don't think about a black cat. What's the first thing you see in your mind's eye?

This can be used to great effect when using conversational hypnosis as you can probably imagine, whist seeming to be having one conversation with the conscious you can be saying something completely different to the subconscious.

It is very sensitive to tone of voice. If you change the inflections of a word during a conversation the subconscious hangs on it.

It doesn't matter if the word I'd spoken with more emphasis or less, louder or softer, shorter or longer. In each case if it is out of sync with the regular rhythm of a conversation the subconscious picks up on it.

We hear this all the time a good example is when politicians speak. Listen to them, they use pauses and different inflections in their voices for emphasis. It's almost imperceptible it almost seems part of their character.

Be warned IT IS NOT, it is calculated and deliberate.

The same goes for how they use their body language as will be revealed.

The subconscious loves itself. It likes to see itself in others. The more alike a person appears to the subconscious the more it will like that person.

It's a safety feature. It is buried deep down in our animal brain, we see the same animal as ourselves we are relaxed, no real threat except perhaps in mating season, the animal sees a predator and it will experience fear. If however it sees prey it will see opportunity.

The subconscious thinks like a small child. It does not have guile what exists in the subconscious just is.

We see this in phobias or bad habits as

mentioned above, all the time. No matter how much the conscious reasons with itself that spiders are smaller than us and that they cannot harm us. The subconscious, like a four year old, simply says, "but I am frightened of spiders".

It also means that it Likes direction

The subconscious likes or more realistically needs direction. Because of this it is a very simple thing to shepherd it in any positive direction.

The subconscious and conscious alike loves the sound of its own name. It is a very easy way to disarm the conscious and allow communication with the subconscious.

Because of the childlike nature of the

subconscious when you use its name it gets the message that you are a friend because we are being so familiar.

Another way to allay the conscious and open up a direct line to the subconscious is by using Slight confusion allows message to filter through.

That's the basics out of the way.

STEP ONE

Step one in using covert hypnosis or hidden persuasion techniques is how you present to your target.

Your body will send unconscious messages out to anyone you communicate with. The subconscious of the target will pick up on these messages and respond accordingly. The thing about body language signals is that genuine feelings are hard to cover up.

Even if you mask or hide your genuine feelings, as we all do, it is the initial half a second that is read by another human being. This is why you instinctively like people sometimes before you have even met them, or conversely dislike them.

So how do you make sure your body language comes across as genuine? The answer of course is that you will genuinely have to like the person. Don't try to fake it you will be found out.

Now you are probably laughing. How do you genuinely like someone you don't even know yet?

Well you have to go there first.

Try this trick and once you know it works do it all the time.

Sit quietly for a second and think about someone you really love. Someone you love without reservation, a child, parent, wife or husband.

Now as you think about that person let yourself feel whatever you feel. You should have very positive emotions. Allow the feeling to build, experience it at every level and through every sense. Hear their voice, see them, experience what they smell like, everything about them. You need to feel it rather than think it.

Once you've experienced that you need to create that same feeling every time you communicate with someone. That is if you want to persuade someone you need to be this way with them.

To do this you will set what is known as an anchor, whilst you are feeling the great feelings do something unique, like touch your finger and thumb together.

Practice a few times until you notice that each time you touch your finger and thumb together you re-experience the positive emotions.

Every time you meet someone touch your finger and thumb together. When you are in this emotional state your body will reflect this in minute detail to the other persons subconscious.

Without doing anything else your interactions with others will improve.

Start points

Whenever you meet someone new especially your target you need a start position. You cannot leave anything to chance, you can of course use conversational hypnosis at any point with anyone but it will be more difficult if the target has preconceptions.

You need to create in them the preconceptions you desire.

The best start position is somewhere between Parallel to forty five degrees turning gradually, Eventually facing the target. This creates a non threatening stance but at the same time showing interest and willingness to engage.

Open and serene

Your general body projection should be open and embracing whilst at the same time you should come across as a leader.

This is quite a complex thing to achieve and must be practiced.

We are not going through every expression and pose, that is far beyond the scope of this book, I suggest you read the excellent "Body Language Exposed by Daryo Nagari", What we are going to go through is a few body language signals that you can use at specific times.

If you have used the aforementioned go there first then you will have a good starting facial expression.

This will be an almost smile, not a false smile but the beginnings of a genuine smile.

The sides of your lips will be slightly higher than the middle. Your eyes will have a soft glow about them and they will have a slight crinkle on the outside of the eye socket.

As for the rest of your body keep movement to a minimum.

If you are a very arm wavy expressive type then learn to restrain yourself.

You will need your body language to have real meaning when you use it so if you minimise your movement now it will have more effect and influence when you do.

Commander

Another thing is you must appear to be a natural leader.

Here is a list of some of the things you should aim for

Head up. Back straight

Torso exposed

When appropriate inside of the arms exposed.

Hands in a neutral position. This means no tension in them.

When saying negative things palms down and gently make a downward motion.

When encouraging positivity palms up with a slight cupping, moving the hands up and down gently.

Do not put your hands behind your back or in your pockets.

Keep your head as still as possible.

When listening tilt your head slightly.

If you use these basic guidelines you will have created a certain amount of trust between yourself and your target subconscious.

We now want to take that baseline trust and create rapport.

Creating rapport means creating a bond.

Now you must show the target that you are the same as them remember we like ourselves. This is quite a simple thing to do, whilst keeping your baseline body pose you must 'mirror'

Mirroring is a technique whereby you sort of copy what your target does beware though not to literally copy or mimic them. It's about doing similar things to them subtly and in a timely fashion.

For instance if your target picks up a glass and takes a drink, wait for a second or two then make a similar movement, perhaps put your hand to your chin for a brief rub or scratch. If they lean towards you slightly again wait for a second and then shift towards them.

Be careful not to just copy them since this will be noticed as a negative by the subconscious. The target will see it as a predatory move, much like a big cat tracking and stalking its prey,

If you want to witness two people in complete rapport go to a bar and watch two good friends together.

You won't have to ask if they're good friends it will be blatantly obvious to you now you know what you are looking for.

Once they are engrossed in conversation you will see that they virtually mirror each other move for move. It's like watching a tennis match! One will lean in and then the other follows. One will drink and again the other follows and it's not just one sided. Perhaps the other person will fold their arms and will be copied by the person who'd previously led.

Match

Along with mirroring you need to match them at a subconscious level this means moving along with them. Imagine you are walking along the street having a conversation with someone and suddenly they begin to walk at twice your speed and you stay at the same pace.

Your pace would be mismatched meaningful communication would be impossible.

When we refer to matching we mean that we would be moving at the same pace with regard to rapport the easiest way to match is to speak the same language as your target.

By speaking the same language I do not mean dialect. I refer to speaking in a manner that they think. Confused? Don't be.

Matching speech type

We all think in different ways some of us think visually this means that we picture things in our minds.

Others think auditory this is to say that they think in sounds

Finally we have the kinetic thinkers these are the tactile and emotional thinkers.

Determining how someone thinks is quite a simple exercise. You need to ask them questions and then observe closely how they reply.

Visual thinkers tend to speak quickly. When considering a question they will look up. They may look either left or right at the same time this is because we access memories and imagination in different ways.

Those that think auditory will keep their eyes level when they look either left or right.

Emotional or kinetic thinkers tend to look down. And they also speak slowly and deliberately.

A good way to remember this is:

Down is looking at the body, where we feel and

Sideways is looking at the ears, where we hear

And up is looking at a wall as if looking at pictures.

A large part of matching is done by listening. How do they express themselves what language do they use. Do they swear a lot do they take long pauses? What descriptive words do they use?

Listening has an added bonus, whilst you are studying the target you will appear to be interested in what they have to say.

Watch two people having difficulties in their relationship. The wife accuses the husband of not communicating with her. The husband on the other hand counters that they talk all the time. When you delve deeper you will almost always find that what they both actually mean is the other doesn't listen.

Now with this information you need to speak to them in the language their subconscious understands.

With visual communicators use words like look see, view, look, bright, colours etc

Auditory communicators should be spoken to using words like hear loud quiet, sounds

And kinetic communicators words like feel sense touch, sense.

Incidentally, using the word sense, for example "I sense something is wrong." Has a powerful effect on the targets mind.

The subconscious will read it as if you are intuitive and empathetic to them. It's a great word to use even with all types of communicators not just kinetic types.

Use their words

Also use their own words back at them. If you are having a conversation with someone and they use the word *'large'* to describe something don't use the word *'big'* in your own reference to the same object or subject, their subconscious childlike mind will take it to be contradictory and rapport will be difficult.

If you use their word *'large'* their subconscious thinks aha that's the same and remember **same is good.**

STEP TWO

Cold read

Start with random seeming stuff, and get steadily more personal.

We move now to the part where we want our target to think or feel that we understand them as a person.

To do this we use random statements known as Barnum statements.

Whether you believe in psychics or not there are some so called mediums or clairvoyants out there who are con artists.

They use a technique called cold reading they

make statements which seem to be quite specific but are actually very global they watch for shifts in body language and expressions on their victims then they adjust and or continue with further statements until they seem to be telling the victim facts about their life which no stranger would know.

Of course the victim then feels as though the medium has deep knowledge about them this is a step further than liking ourselves.

This feels as though the medium knows them better than themselves.

The Forer effect is the ability for an individual to make something vague and general fit their personal situation.

So we use a similar technique to build upon the

foundation of rapport to the next level on the way to covertly influencing or hypnotising someone.

These are the standard Barnum statements:

They can be used individually or together.

You have a great need for others people to like and admire you

You have a tendency to be critical of yourself

You have a great deal of unused capacity which you have not turned to your advantage

While you have some personality weakness, you are generally able to compensate for them

Your sexual adjustment has presented problems for you

Disciplined and controlled outside, you tend to be worry some and insecure inside.

At times you have serious doubts as to whether you have made the right decision or done the right thing.

You prefer a certain amount of change and variety and become dissatisfied when hemmed in by restriction and limitations.

You pride yourself as an independent thinker and do not accept others statements without satisfactory proof.

You have found it unwise to be too frank when revealing yourself to others.

At times you are extrovert, affable, sociable, while at other times you are introvert, wary and reserved

Some of your aspirations tend to be pretty unrealistic

Security is one of your major goals in life.

You don't have to look too closely to see that all of these statements have been relevant to just about all of us at certain times during our lives. And if they're not,'take them with you' *that's my little joke!*

You see though, to the unsuspecting target being in rapport with you it feels like you understand them. It's not unusual to hear statements to that effect.

He knew me better than I know myself or he understands me on a level that no one ever has before.

Once you have peppered the victim with these general statements you move on to more specific things sing their dress and mannerisms to make educated guesses about them.

Own statements

Another thing to do is to modify or even create your own catchall statements. That way you will seem even more genuine.

STEP THREE

Using your words.

Combining all the following elements, metaphors, stories, embedded commands, power words, tonality, voice, inflections, homophones, and triggers.

Metaphors.

Some people like to tell stories loaded with metaphors in an Ericksonian style. Stories to influence the target we are going to use what are known as stories that grab them

Embedded commands.

These are orders or commands that are given directly to the subconscious mind they are often hidden in seemingly innocuous sentences for instance you could say something like

'In a moment you might find **you will drift off to sleep**. Now in your own time let that feeling wash over you'.

Power words.

Power words these are words which appeal to the subconscious mind at a base level. These are words and statements which, as you would imagine have a powerful effect on the subconscious mind.

Power words are always used in the construction of embedded command statements.

Here are some examples. The more you think

about language the more you will realise there
are hundreds more of these power words and
phrases

As

As if

Attractive

Beautiful

Because

Calm

Can

Comfortable

Command

Completely

Could

Deeper

Demand

Down

Drift

Drowsy

Excellent

Feel

Gently

Go

Good

Great

Hypnosis

Imagine

Intense

Just

Like

Know

Love

Need

Notice

Now

Pleasant

Realise

Relax

Safe

Sleep

Sleepy

Slowly

Softly

Soothing

Tension

Trance

Unconsciously

Want

We

When

Will

Would

Tonality and voice inflections.

We use tone inflections this is when we slightly change the tone of our voice at the point when we say the relevant words.

Slight of tongue.

We can use whole words or fragments of words

Misspeak words or use words that are similar to an ordinary word in the conversation but are different slightly.

A good example of this is the fun countdown. It can be used as a deepener or an emergence in regular hypnosis. It goes something like this.

Counting down through five, for this can take you deeper and deeper forward (four) three just takes you to (two) one.

Homophones.

Use homophones these are words which seem the like right word but with different meanings. We use these to confuse and send the message

Eye   I

Bare   bear

Brake   break

Buy   by

Coarse   course

Dear   deer

Hear   here

Hole   whole

Hour   our

Knight   night

Know   no

Made   maid

Mail   male

49

One   won

Pair   pear

Peace piece

Real   reel

Right   write

Root   route

Sail   sale

Sea   see

Seam seem

Sew   so

Shore sure

Son   sun

Suite sweet

Their there

.

To too

Toe   tow

Waist waste

Wait   weight

Way   weigh

Weak week

Wear where

Triggers.

Use triggers to link feelings with commands. As described in the going there first section in the earlier chapter.

This time however you set a trigger in the target. It's very simple to do whenever you make a statement you make a movement or signal. Eventually the subconscious links the two, then you can simply use the signal to evoke the action you require.

A good example is the one used by pickup artists. When talking to their victim about feeling good they touch their arm or leg or anywhere. Then as they increase the emotional response, they move their hand.

When to break away.

Another seemingly counter intuitive action is the breakaway.

We spend so much time creating rapport it is very tempting to maintain the contact, in fact when you try this kind of persuasion technique you may well be fearful that breaking rapport will break the spell.

In a one off encounter this is very true, however if you wish to use covert hypnosis on someone over an extended period at some point you will have to say goodbye and resume later.

Timing these breaks is of utmost importance.

Whilst your target is still interested in what you

are saying and in being in your company that is when you break. It leaves the business incomplete in the victims subconscious. It will be eager to meet you again to resume the rapport.

If you do not make this breakaway things will go badly wrong very quickly. The rapport you have so carefully created will be broken.

You see you will outstay your welcome, you will exhaust the conversation and the victims subconscious will become bored with you, you have nothing fresh to say.

Once you break it gives the victim time to settle and think and ask itself questions about you. Then on your next encounter it wants to know more about you. There exists an element of mystery which keeps the interest alive.

www.ingramcontent.com/pod-product-compliance
Lightning Source LLC
Chambersburg PA
CBHW070458290526
45790CB00003B/1001